THE

BEGINNER'S

GUIDE

TO

CPP DISABILITY

How to Request, Win, and
Keep Your Benefits

Table of Contents

ABOUT THE AUTHOR

Hello.

I'm David Brannen, an occupational therapist who became a disability lawyer to help those who need CPP benefits. I created Resolute Legal, a national law firm, to focus on representing people with their claims.

Every Canadian with a disability should have access to justice, and I've represented thousands over the past fifteen years. As a past president of the Atlantic Provinces Trial Lawyers Association and a member of the Ontario Trial Lawyers Association and American Association for Justice, I've had the opportunity to speak to thousands more about these issues.

I'm no superhero, just a normal guy living in New Brunswick with his wife, kids, and dogs. But you shouldn't need a superhero to win your case. You do need information, though, and I'm here to help.

PREFACE

In early 2013, an upset woman asked me for help with her CPP disability appeal. At the time, I was leaving my career as a personal injury lawyer and launching a law firm to focus on disability-related claims. Another lawyer knew this and referred the woman to me.

This woman had seen her claim denied three times (the last time with legal representation), but she had just gotten a letter allowing her to appeal to the newly formed *Social Security Tribunal*. This letter gave her one more chance, so she desperately wanted to win this time.

Although I had experience with disability claims, I had yet to represent anyone in a CPP disability appeal. I told her this, but she hired me anyways. When I reviewed her claim, I saw that she had evidence gaps and wasn't presenting a compelling story, so a *decision-maker* (the adjudicator or tribunal judge) couldn't easily see her situation and approve her claim.

After I sent in the missing evidence and adjusted her story, Service Canada offered to approve her claim before the hearing.

This case taught me a lesson that has held up in the hundreds of CPP disability cases I've worked since then: Yes, you can lose a winnable case if you don't present the right evidence and tell your story in the right way.

So I wrote this book to teach you how to present your claims and appeals properly. You must know as much as you can about the process and what you need to do to boost your chances of success.

INTRODUCTION

Welcome to the Beginners Guide to CPP (Canada Pension Plan) Disability. In this guide, you'll learn how to apply for benefits and avoid the most common mistakes that result in denials. My goal is to give you the best chance for success.

By the end of this book you will:

- Know if you qualify for CPP disability benefits.

- Understand how to apply.

- Know who decides your claim and how.

- Be able to present your disability properly to the decision-makers.

- Discover the most common reasons for denial and what to do in each situation.

- Know how to appeal a denial.

- Be able to handle issues that come up after approval.

- Understand your choices for representation.

CPP disability benefits exist to help Canadians who can no longer work because of permanent disability. In 2017, the CPP disability program paid 4.3 billion dollars to approximately 335,000 beneficiaries and 83,000 children of beneficiaries. To qualify, you must meet the CPP requirements.

I wrote this book because too many deserving *claimants* (people applying for benefits) lose their benefits for technical reasons, even if they meet all requirements. Yes, you can lose a winnable case if you don't follow the rules or present your claim poorly. Missing deadlines, lacking the right evidence, or failing to present a compelling story almost always results in denials. Unfortunately, many claimants learn the hard way.

As a beginner's guide, this book presumes that you have very little knowledge or experience with the CPP disability program. As a practical guide, this book does not qualify as a legal textbook. It only points out key issues so you can make better decisions and improve your chances of success.

In Chapter One, you get an overview of the CPP disability program and its requirements. Read it carefully if you haven't applied yet or want to know if you qualify for CPP disability.

Chapter Two covers the application process. We review things you can do before you apply to improve your chances of success, and then take you step by step through the process.

In Chapter Three, we talk about what happens to your claim after you send it in. You'll learn about the people who approve or deny claims, the process they use, and the evidence they find convincing.

Chapter Four covers issues related to denials and appeals. You'll find out the common reasons for denial and how to appeal a denial.

Chapter Five will tell you what happens after you win your claim. We address common questions about payment schedules, taxation, other income sources, and returning to work.

In Chapter Six, we cover representation. This includes the different kinds of representatives and when it makes sense to hire one.

Finally, keep in mind that the CPP disability program changes, like everything else. Just as this book was about to go out, the federal government announced that it would spend $253 million over the next five years (2019 to 2023) to make changes to the Social Security Tribunal. As an author, you don't want to hear such news when you just finished a book on the subject! However, the planned changes will not affect most of what you read in this book.

The most important change will affect how the Social Security Tribunal handles appeal hearings. A tribunal judge currently decides these hearings, but this will change to a panel of three people. I expect this panel to include a lawyer, a health professional, and a member of the public. As explained in Chapter Four, I also expect changes to deadlines for submitting documents and how the panel holds the hearings. All of these changes will happen over time, so some people will continue to fall under the current system, while other people will begin in the new system. You can stay up to date on the changes at *www.resolutelegal.ca/cpp-disability-benefits* or by signing up for our email updates about the CPP disability program.

OVERVIEW OF THE PROGRAM

What are Canada Pension Plan (CPP) Disability Benefits?

Canada Pension Plan (CPP) disability benefits are monthly payments made to those who can no longer work because of a disability. The Canada Pension Plan pays several other benefits, but this guide will only review disability benefits. To qualify, you must meet the age, contribution, and disability requirements. If you do, Service Canada will pay you every month for as long as you continue to meet the requirements or until you turn sixty-five. If you qualify and have dependent children, then Service Canada will make an extra payment for each child.

Eligibility

First, you must be between eighteen and sixty-five years old. Second, you must pay enough into the program. Third, you must have a "*severe* and *prolonged*" disability as defined by the program. Let's look at each requirement in more detail.

AGE

You must be between the ages of eighteen and sixty-five at the time of your application. However, people between sixty and sixty-five can't get

CPP disability and CPP retirement at the same time. If you've gotten CPP retirement for fifteen months or less, then you may qualify to have your retirement converted to disability.

CONTRIBUTION

You must meet strict *contribution requirements*. You may have paid into the program, but if you didn't pay the proper amount, you won't qualify.

To meet the contribution requirement, you must have made minimum qualifying payments in four of the last six years or three of the last six if you contributed for at least twenty-five years. You calculate these figures using the years leading up to the date you became unable to work due to disability, called your *date of onset*, not the date you apply for benefits. If you don't meet this requirement based on your past work, you may qualify for credits from one of the following situations:

- Becoming legally separated or divorced *(credit splitting)*
- Leaving work to become the primary caregiver for at least one child under the age of seven *(child-rearing dropout provision)*
- Paying into a national pension plan in another country *(pension credits from other countries)*

Credit Splitting

If you separated or divorced from a spouse, then you can apply for a division of unadjusted pensionable earnings (DUPE), commonly called credit splitting. This practice results in the higher-earning spouse yielding credits to the lower-earning spouse to help the lower earner meet contribution requirements.

Child-Rearing Dropout Provision

If you left work to become a primary caregiver for a child under the age of seven, then you may qualify for credits under the child-rearing dropout provision. The Canadian government created this provision to avoid penalizing parents who leave their jobs to raise their children. If you qualify, you get credits for the years you spent in primary childcare instead of employment.

This increases your potential payment amount and extends your qualifying period.

Pension Credits from Other Countries

If you ever worked outside of Canada and paid into another country's pension plan, then those credits may transfer to the Canada Pension Plan. Canada has agreements with many countries that allow this transfer, and these credits have the same value as those you get in Canada. Transferring credits to the Canada Pension Plan has the dual benefit of increasing your contribution period and your benefits payments.

DISABILITY

You must have a "severe and prolonged disability" as defined by the CPP disability program. "Severe" means it must make you unable to gain or hold a steady job. "Prolonged" means that a doctor has said your disability will last indefinitely or result in death.

Keep in mind that severity is about your ability to work rather than the medical condition itself. Even if you have a serious condition, you must show that this condition prevents you from gaining or holding a steady job. Only then will CPP cover your disability.

Service Canada considers the following to determine "severe and prolonged" disabilities:

- The effects the disability has on you and whether they'll worsen
- Your ability to work and how it may change
- Whether you have done all you can do to stay in the workforce
- Whether you have complied with all treatment recommendations
- The effects the treatment will have on your ability to work
- Statements from you and health professionals involved in your case
- Existence of multiple medical conditions
- Personal characteristics

We'll discuss these factors in more detail in the section on proving your disability.

Date of Onset and Minimum Qualifying Period

Your *date of onset* (DOO) must happen during the time when you met your contribution requirements, called the *minimum qualifying period (MQP)*. You can meet all other requirements but still not qualify if your date of onset didn't happen during your MQP.

In my experience, few understand DOOs and MQPs, resulting in mistakes during the application and appeals process. Claimants often use a DOO that falls outside their MQP and don't present evidence of disability, treatment, and work efforts during the MQP. So let's try to make these complex subjects easier.

DATE OF ONSET (DOO)

You must pick a date when your disability became "severe and prolonged" as defined by the program. Even if your disability happened gradually, the law requires a calendar date to stand as the point where your disability prevented you from steady work. A traumatic injury event often makes the DOO obvious, although not always (some go back to work and then feel effects from the event later). However, a chronic illness makes your DOO more difficult to pinpoint.

And also remember that your DOO doesn't stand for the day your disability started, but the day it became "severe and prolonged" as defined by the program. This date may line up with your last day of work, but it could happen before you stopped working. Choosing the right DOO can make or break your claim.

MINIMUM QUALIFYING PERIOD (MQP)

The MQP seems to be the most difficult concept to grasp. It's a bit like car insurance. Car insurance will only cover an accident if it happened during a period when you paid your premiums, right?

Well, the CPP disability program will only make disability payments if your disability started during a time when you paid into CPP.

You pay CPP on each paycheque as a mandatory payroll tax, deducted by your employer. That means you should have CPP coverage as long as your CPP tax came out of your paycheque in four of the last six years, or three of the past six years if you have twenty-five years of contributions. The MQP's end date is often two years after your last year of CPP contributions.

For example, let's say you suffered from chronic pain and stopped work on November 5, 2016. If you paid into CPP from 2013 to 2016, then your MQP should run until December 31, 2018. In this case, you'd need to prove your DOO happened before December 31, 2018, during your MQP.

LATE APPLICATION PROVISION

If you apply for CPP disability benefits after your MQP expires, Service Canada will say your application is late. Applying late doesn't mean you lose your benefits. It just means that you need to prove that your DOO happened before the end of your MQP. Canadian law includes a *late application provision* to allow you to apply for CPP disability after your MQP expires.

For example, Mary's application is dated May 25, 2018. She gets a letter saying that her application is "late" because her minimum qualifying period expired on December 31, 2016 (outside of her MQP). Service Canada will then check Mary's claim under the late application provision and figure out if her DOO happened before December 31, 2016, during her MQP. If so, then Service Canada would move on to decide if Mary meets the other requirements.

However, if Service Canada finds that Mary's DOO happened after December 31, 2016, it will deny the claim as not meeting contribution requirements. With the right evidence and arguments, Mary could have this decision overturned on appeal.

Benefits for Children

If you win your claim for disability benefits and have dependent children, then they too will each qualify for a benefit. You apply for children's benefits as part of the regular application. Qualifying children must be under the age of eighteen or be a full-time student between the ages of eighteen and twenty-four.

The children's benefit is $244.64 per month per child (in 2018) and increases each year by inflation. The payment usually goes to the parent or guardian, but children older than eighteen may get the benefit directly.

KEY TAKEAWAYS FOR THIS CHAPTER

♦ CPP disability is a federal program that pays a monthly benefit to qualified people.

♦ To qualify for CPP disability payments, you must meet the age, contribution, and disability requirements.

♦ If you don't meet the contribution requirements, you may still qualify by using credit splitting, credits from other countries, or the child-rearing provision.

♦ If you send in a late application, you may still qualify for benefits if you can prove your DOO happened during your MQP.

♦ If you qualify for CPP disability benefits, your dependent children may also qualify for the CPP children's benefits.

APPLYING

Before You Begin

Early action can improve your chances of winning. Above all, make sure you have accurate and detailed records of your disability from your health professionals. That means you must go to your regular appointments, describe your symptoms and problems carefully, and show that you've tried everything your doctors suggest, even if you disagreed with some of the suggestions. You should tell your doctors how your medical condition affects your work and then ask for their suggestions.

The better your records track your condition and treatment(s), the more likely you are to have your claim approved. You want clinical notes and records that show how you tried to get better and stay at work. If your medical records don't have this information, you'll have a hard time getting your claim approved, even if you are disabled.

How to Apply

STEP 1: LEARN THE PROCESS

Knowing as much as you can about the program and the process will help you make better decisions and increase your chances of success. You don't want your claim denied on technical grounds when you're legitimately disabled and meet all the criteria for payment.

STEP 2: GET THE PACKAGE

The CPP Application Package includes the official forms you need to fill out. Service Canada will only accept paper applications, so make sure you get paper copies of the forms. You can pick them up at any Service Canada office or download and print them from Service Canada's CPP website, or at www.resolutelegal.ca/cpp-disability-benefits.

STEP 3: FILL OUT THE FORMS

We recommend a practice version first, like a rehearsal. Fill out a copy of the form to find out how much information you can fit in the boxes. If you only have one copy, then write your answers on a separate sheet. Once you feel comfortable with the answers you've written, then you can transfer them to the form you'll mail in.

The form contains several sections:

- Personal information (name, birthdate, address, social insurance number)
- Contributions to the Canada Pension Plan
- Details of your medical condition and abilities
- Information about your doctor or nurse practitioner
- Review of your work
- Information on your children
- Banking information for direct deposit if approved
- Consent for Service Canada to get personal information

- Declaration and signature

These topics can change over time, so make sure you alway⌐ recent version of the forms.

The most challenging section focuses on your medical condition. Take special care when describing your disability and how long you've had it. You may need to consider your contribution history and minimum qualifying period.

Also, you need to take care when listing what medical problems stop you from working. If you apply under the late application provision, then you must focus on the problems that stopped you from working **during** your MQP. If you focus on problems that started or worsened **after** that period, then you may get denied.

You have to rate your abilities as well, often phrased as "ability level on most days" on the form. Make sure either your answers match what your medical records say or you have good explanations for whatever doesn't match. Under each section, you can give more information, and you should. If your disability or impairment varies from day to day, then mention that.

For the sections on your work, think carefully about the changes you, your employer, or your co-workers had to make because of your disability. In my experience, claimants approach this too narrowly, focusing on official changes in duties or positions. You should discuss all changes you made to your employment, even those not officially accepted by your employer.

You may have made small tweaks to your routine to cope with your medical problems, tweaks that your boss didn't notice. Co-workers may have given you unofficial help. You may have avoided certain tasks, reorganized your workspace, or worked from home. Answer this section in as much detail as possible.

Once you're happy with your answers, fill out the official form to send to Service Canada. The rehearsal will keep your final application form neat and organized.

STEP 4: WORK WITH YOUR DOCTOR ON THE MEDICAL REPORT

Service Canada won't consider your application complete until it gets your application form and the medical report form. You have to get your doctor to fill out the medical report and return it to Service Canada. Although your doctor has to fill out the form, it's your responsibility to make sure this gets done.

Unfortunately, some doctors do better with this form than others. Some don't take enough time to fill out the report properly. Some don't understand it but feel too embarrassed to say so.

Sometimes doctors have mistaken beliefs about the level of disability a person must have to qualify. Many well-meaning doctors believe their patients aren't disabled enough, when in fact their patients do meet the criteria. Unfortunately, some doctors become defensive when patients try to enlighten them.

And some doctors may not fill out the report the way you want if they believe you're not following their treatment plans. In this case, you need to do your best to cooperate with your doctor and the treatment plans.

If you suspect you may have problems with your medical report, then you need to have an honest talk with your doctor. But don't come on too strong or you'll push your doctor away.

Finally, don't get stuck on trying to get your doctor to say, "My patient suffers from a severe and prolonged disability" or a similar phrase. This sentence won't automatically get your claim approved, because Service Canada focuses on substance over form. Your doctor needs to describe your condition in detail as well as your current and future treatment plans, your participation and your condition's response to treatment, and how your condition will likely progress.

STEP 5: MAIL YOUR APPLICATION

Once you finish your part of the application, mail it to Service Canada immediately. Your doctor can send the medical report later. If you mail your application right away, Service Canada can begin to process your claim and complete the process once your medical report arrives. You can also send more information after you send your form in, so get that form sent!

Remember, you must mail paper copies of the completed forms to the processing centre for your province. Service Canada won't accept applications by email or fax. Service Canada won't accept applications by courier, either, but will accept applications sent by Canada Post express mail. We recommend you use express mail.

And don't drop off your application at a local Service Canada office, even if someone there accepts it. That someone will do nothing more than drop it in the mail for you, or use some internal courier service, and may forget it or lose it before then.

STEP 6: FOLLOW UP

After you send your application, find out whether your doctor sent the medical report. Your application isn't complete until Service Canada gets the medical report from your doctor.

STEP 7: WAIT

At this point, you can only wait for approval or denial. Service Canada usually issues a decision within four months from the date your application was complete. Don't worry if it takes longer, as delays often have more to do with backlogs in Service Canada's system than problems in the claims.

Your application may take longer if Service Canada needs more information from you or others involved in the claim, like your doctor or employer. Although such requests may stretch out your claim, you should stay calm and cooperate as much as possible.

KEY TAKEAWAYS FOR THIS CHAPTER

♦ Your health records must document your medical condition, disability, treatment, and problems with work before you apply for CPP disability benefits.

♦ You must apply for CPP disability using the official paper application forms.

♦ Your description of your medical symptoms and limitations must match what your medical records say, or you may lose credibility.

♦ Explain all tweaks or changes you made to your work routine because of your medical condition or disability.

♦ Send your application using Canada Post express mail. Don't try to use a courier or drop it off at a local Service Canada office.

CLAIM DECISIONS

Who Decides Your Claim?

Your claim is decided by three types of decision-makers: medical adjudicators, tribunal judges, and tribunal panels. These decision-makers have unique characteristics, experiences, and perspectives, and that means that they make decisions differently and value different things. You need to present your claim differently depending on who'll decide. Claimants new to the process tend to focus on what they find convincing, rather than what the decision-makers would find convincing. Don't make this mistake!

MEDICAL ADJUDICATORS

At the application and *reconsideration* stages, a *medical adjudicator* employed by Service Canada makes the decisions. These health professionals (almost always nurses) have training on handling disability claims for the CPP program. Remember that they'll focus more on the medical than the legal parts of claims. And just like everyone else with busy desk jobs, they have bosses to keep happy and an endless stream of work every day.

TRIBUNAL JUDGES

At the Social Security Tribunal stage, a *tribunal member*, usually a lawyer with CPP training, will decide your claim. Tribunal members serve as judges, some for CPP disability hearings and others for appeals. They rely mostly on medical evidence when deciding a claim but will also consider legal arguments in favour of approval or denial. Like medical adjudicators, tribunal members have a constant flow of new appeals and pressure to hold hearings and issue decisions quickly.

THREE-PERSON TRIBUNAL PANELS

On March 21, 2019, the government announced that tribunal hearings will soon have a three-person panel rather than a tribunal judge. By panel, I mean a group of people appointed to perform a service, like a jury panel. I expect this panel will include a lawyer, a health professional, and a member of the community. Similar to a jury, these three people will sit together to hear a person's appeal and will then make a joint decision to approve or deny the claim. Keep in mind the different backgrounds and perspectives of the panel members when presenting your case. You need to present your case differently to a three-person panel than to a single tribunal judge.

How They Decide

The CPP disability program doesn't have an official process that decision-makers must follow. However, Service Canada has guidelines for its medical adjudicators, called the Canada Pension Plan Adjudication Framework, on the Service Canada's CPP disability website. You can review the framework to understand how a medical adjudicator will handle your claim or appeal.

Tribunal judges and panels don't have to follow Service Canada's Adjudication Framework. Although we don't know exactly what process a judge or panel uses to decide a claim, I created the following steps based on the Adjudication Framework and my experience with hearings. This section will give you some sense of what adjudicators, judges, and panel members consider when deciding your claim.

STEP 1: HAVE YOU PAID ENOUGH INTO THE CPP PROGRAM?

Have you paid enough into the program to qualify for CPP disability benefits? Many claims fail here because the claimants never paid enough into the program.

Even if you paid enough, you only have a set amount of time where you can qualify, and you still have to prove your date of onset (DOO) happened during the minimum qualifying period (MQP). You may have had coverage years ago, but as long as you had the appropriate period of coverage, the decision-maker will move to the next steps.

STEP 2: DO YOU HAVE A JOB?

Some people apply for disability benefits while they work full- or part-time jobs. Although you may make less than before, the program may consider you able to do substantially gainful employment.

"Substantially gainful employment" means you earn the same amount as the maximum CPP disability pension, $1,335.83 per month or $16,029.96 per year in 2018. These amounts increase at the rate of inflation. If your job pays you at least this much, then you don't qualify.

However, in some rare cases, called *benevolent employment situations*, a person holds a job and gets a paycheque from an employer out of friendship or charity.

In this case, you can qualify, but you'll have to stop receiving that paycheque if Service Canada approves your disability claim.

STEP 3: HOW DOES YOUR CONDITION AFFECT YOUR ABILITY TO WORK?

The decision-makers will review your records for evidence of symptoms or impairments that would affect your ability to work. No matter how serious your doctor says your condition is, the symptoms and impairments must stop you from doing substantially gainful work for you to get CPP benefits.

STEP 4: CAN YOU WORK IF YOU HAVE HELP?

Even if you have serious symptoms and impairments, the decision-makers must consider whether you can continue your job if you had changes to your work, like going part-time or changing your duties. The decision-makers will deny a claim if it looks like you could continue work with such changes or if your employer offered the changes and you didn't try them. They may also deny your clam if you never asked about changing duties. To win a claim, you must ask for workplace accommodations and try any changes offered, even if you believe they won't help.

STEP 5: CAN YOU WORK A DIFFERENT JOB?

Regardless of how much you liked your old job, or how well you did it, if you can't do it now, you have to try other jobs. You must prove that you can't do enough work for a paycheque. Show that you made good faith efforts in other, easier jobs but can't perform them because of your impairment. Again, you have to try even if you don't believe your efforts will succeed. If you don't try, it may look like you **won't** rather than you **can't**.

The decision-makers consider other jobs in the national economy that you could do, given your age, education, experience, skills, and impairment. If they decide you have the ability to do another job, then they'll deny your claim. Please note that location doesn't matter. If you can work in another city or province, they'll deny your claim because you have work available.

STEP 6: HAVE YOU FOLLOWED YOUR DOCTOR'S ORDERS?

The decision-makers also have to consider if your disability has become severe because you haven't followed a treatment plan or have refused treatment altogether. Many claims have "failure to reasonably comply with medical advice" as the reason for denial. Don't leave room for them to believe you refused reasonable advice.

If you want to boost your chances of having your claim approved, you must cooperate completely with your treatment professionals, even those you disagree with. You have to at least try so the doctor can rule it out.

The following situations qualify as failure to comply with medical advice:

- Refusing to try medications from a treating doctor or nurse practitioner
- Stopping a medication trial against medical advice
- Refusing to attend a rehabilitation program
- Not showing up for treatment programs
- Withdrawing from treatment programs prematurely or being discharged because of too many "no shows"
- Not making reasonable efforts to find public funding for treatments
- Refusing or failing to go to referred specialists

Decision-makers see it as your duty to make every effort to improve your condition before you can get disability benefits, and they only accept professional opinions. If you decide to stop or refuse treatment based on your own beliefs or research, you'll lose your claim. You can only stop or refuse treatment if another doctor recommends that you do so. If you feel that your current treatment won't work, you must get another doctor to support you in writing.

STEP 7: DOES YOUR DISABILITY QUALIFY AS "PROLONGED"?

According to the CPP definition, a "prolonged" disability will impair you for life or the foreseeable future. CPP disability doesn't cover temporary impairment, no matter how severe. If an upcoming surgery or completion of a rehabilitation program can give your disability an end date, then you won't qualify.

Proof

Adjudicators, judges, and panel members can only make decisions based on the evidence they see, and certain rules limit what a judge or other decision-maker can see.

That means that tribunal judges and panels can only decide based on proper evidence. You may have facts that prove a point, but if they don't follow the rules then you can't use them. That also means that a judge may rule against you if you don't present all the facts that help you.

These rules apply to claims and appeals. You have to prove your claim using evidence the tribunal judge or panel will accept. Some claimants assume their claims have to be approved because they really can't work. But you absolutely must prove it properly, using the right evidence and presentation. You can make personal statements if you want, but offering medical records and outside opinions will get you a lot farther.

Let's talk about the three most common types of evidence: 1) lay witness evidence, 2) expert evidence, and 3) documents.

LAY WITNESS EVIDENCE

A lay witness testifies based on personal knowledge and life experiences rather than expertise. Lay witnesses can tell the adjudicator or judge what they've noticed about your condition and how it affects your life. To a limited extent, they can also offer conclusions or opinions. Lay witnesses in a CPP case would include you (the applicant), family members, and co-workers.

You can give written statements, or you can swear in and speak at a tribunal hearing. This kind of swearing means that you tell your story under solemn oath to tell only the truth.

Most of these hearings only have one lay witness, the person applying for benefits. This testimony should cover:

- Work and education history.

- Treatments and outcome of treatments.

- How you tried to return work and why you couldn't.

- The nature and extent of symptoms or disability.

- Explanations of any bad facts or discrepancies.

In some situations, it makes sense to have other lay witnesses testify, but only if they focus on critical facts that you (the applicant) can't give. Having witnesses come up just to say they believe you won't help. In fact, it will only annoy the judge or panel members.

Examples of lay witness evidence include:

- Written *submissions* (reports, statements, etc.) from the applicant.

- Statements from the applicant found in medical records or reports.

- Written statements from friends and family.

- Written statements or records from an employer or co-worker.

- Verbal testimony by the applicant at a tribunal hearing.

EXPERT EVIDENCE

An expert witness offers scientific opinion and evidence based on education, training, and credentials. Lay witnesses can give limited opinions and information, but judges expect expert witnesses to give detailed opinions and draw conclusions within their fields of expertise. While health professionals rarely give verbal testimony in a CPP disability case, the court will accept their opinions in medical records and reports.

You need expert evidence to support your claim. You can talk about your symptoms and impairment, but only a health professional can give expert opinions on your diagnosis, treatment, and future outlook. No matter how much research you've done, you don't count as an expert witness in the eyes of the law.

Examples of expert evidence include:

- Medical reports or letters written by health professionals.

- Clinical notes of a health professional.

- Diagnostic imaging and reports.

- Reports covering medical tests and examinations.

- A health professional speaking at a tribunal hearing.

DOCUMENTS

Documents are the most important evidence in a CPP disability case, and medical records are the most important documents. Not having the right document can easily kill a winnable case, and medical records contain expert opinion and lay evidence about your case.

These records open a window into your disability to let the judge or panel members see how it affects you. Your symptoms, ability to work, treatments, and outcomes all should show up here. To find out how your symptoms affected you three years ago, the decision-makers will look to medical records made three years ago rather than what you remember today.

Examples of document evidence include:

- Complete medical files from your doctors.

- Hospital records related to your condition.

- Clinical records and reports from specialists.

- Rehabilitation records from physiotherapists or chiropractors.

- Psychological records.

- Insurance records.

- Employment records, including sick time used, hours worked, and performance evaluations.

- Reports from health professionals addressing key issues or information gaps.

TIMING OF EVIDENCE

If you need to prove something happened, you want to use a document created at that time. Don't rely on your memories or someone else's. Get as much documentation as you can to prove past events or facts, and continue documenting your disability as you continue to experience it. It may change in unexpected ways or times, and you need records of those changes.

SUPPORTING CREDIBILITY

Medical documents will give you some of the best support for your claim, but the decision-makers need to believe you too. In legal settings, credibility refers to a witness's trustworthiness or believability.

A tribunal judge or panel who finds you trustworthy may rule in your favour, even if you have weak documentation to support your claim. And a judge or panel who doesn't trust you won't accept your testimony or give you the benefit of the doubt in uncertain areas, even with good evidence. Credibility gives you an invisible edge, but many applicants never think about this point.

Credibility killers include:

- Contradicting medical records or earlier statements.

- Making excuses or blaming others for problems.

- Criticizing other parties in the claim (even if they deserve it).

- Filing complaints against professionals you see as negative, biased, or unprofessional.

- Using aggressive, sarcastic, or confrontational tones in your testimony.

- Blocking or stalling reasonable requests for information.

- Fighting with doctors over a diagnosis instead of focusing on the disability.
- Acting like a medical expert.
- Complaining about "undeserving" people getting "your" benefits.
- Saying you deserve benefits because you paid into the CPP.

Credibility boosters include:

- Making sure what you say matches the medical records.
- Taking responsibility for bad facts or other problems in your claim.
- Being cooperative and respectful with everyone in the claim.
- Accepting expert medical advice and opinion.
- Not blaming other people or minority groups.
- Making good faith efforts to try all reasonable advice, even if you disagree with it.
- Obvious efforts to keep working.

Your personal beliefs about what makes a person credible don't matter. The decision-makers' beliefs do. This comes back to knowing who will view your claim and how they perceive things.

As a disability lawyer, I've spent a lot of time trying to fix damaged or weak credibility. Unfortunately, some claimants are their own worst enemies and lose benefits, even though they should qualify. Don't be your own worst enemy.

KEY TAKEAWAYS FOR THIS CHAPTER

♦ Your claim is decided by medical adjudicators for applications and reconsiderations and by tribunal judges or panels for tribunal hearings.

♦ When deciding claims, medical adjudicators follow the Canada Pension Plan Adjudication Framework.

♦ When deciding claims, tribunal judges and panels focus on whether you've done all you can to keep working and follow treatment plans.

♦ Medical records or written opinions from doctors or other health professionals are the best kinds of proof.

♦ You must act respectfully and professionally during the course of your claim.

♦ You can lose a winnable case, if you don't handle your claim or appeals properly.

CLAIM DENIALS AND APPEALS

On March 21, 2019, the federal government announced plans to change the Social Security Tribunal. These changes will roll out between 2019 and 2023. During this time, some people will continue under the current process and others will enter the new process.

The government is only changing the Tribunal appeals and has no changes planned for applications or reconsideration appeals. While we don't know all the changes yet, I'll review the current appeals process below and go over the expected changes. We recommend you look for the most up-to-date information for your appeal on the official Service Canada site or at www. resolutelegal.ca/cpp-disability-benefits.

How to Appeal a Denial

If a decision-maker (adjudicator, judge, or panel) denies your claim or makes a decision you don't agree with (like payment amount), you have the right to begin climbing the appeal ladder. You may only need one or two levels, or you may find yourself going through all four:

1. Reconsideration Appeal

2. Appeal to the Social Security Tribunal (General Division)

3. Appeal to the Social Security Tribunal (Appeals Division)

4. Appeal to the Federal Court of Canada

Each level becomes more complex, so you should prepare yourself. The first and second levels focus on your claim and let you fix mistakes you made in earlier appeals, such as evidence gaps. But the third and fourth levels focus on whether your **decision-makers** made a legal mistake or didn't give a fair hearing, so you can't fix any of your own mistakes on those levels. Let's review each level in more detail.

LEVEL 1: RECONSIDERATION APPEAL

If Service Canada denies your claim or stops payments from an approved claim, you'll get a letter explaining why. If you don't agree, then you can apply to have this decision reconsidered. For this appeal, Service Canada assigns a new adjudicator, who may overturn the original decision.

You have multiple steps to go through, but remember, **you must send the official form within ninety days** to ask for the reconsideration. None of the other steps will matter if you're late. Now that you know, we'll review the steps.

Step 1: Identify the deadline

Once you get the letter from Service Canada, you then have ninety days to ask for your reconsideration. That means you need to sit with a calendar and figure out when your ninety days are up, then get your form in before that date.

Step 2: Immediately send the form

Get your reconsideration request form, fill it out, and mail it in immediately. Don't worry about sending information at this point. You can include a note on the form saying that you'll send it later. As soon as Service Canada gets that form, you no longer have to worry about the ninety-day deadline. You can then gather and send more information, even if you go beyond the ninety days.

Step 3: Send the information you need

Once you have that deadline out of the way, you can gather and send in other documents. Medical adjudicators will try to wait for all of your documents before making a decision. But remember, they have deadlines, too. If you take too long, the adjudicator may decide your claim before you send in all your documents. Ask the adjudicator for more time if you're having trouble getting medical files or reports from doctors.

Step 4: Cooperate with requests for more information

After you send in all your documents, the adjudicator may ask for more records from your health professionals or employer. Many adjudicators will order these documents for you and pay any fees to get them. If you have a lawyer or advocate helping you, that person could ask for that information on your behalf, but you may have to do it yourself. Either way, make sure the adjudicator knows you're taking steps to cooperate.

Step 5: Wait

Once you send all your documents, it can take one to three months for the adjudicator to reach a decision. If you don't agree with it, then you can move to the next level, appealing to the General Division of the Social Security Tribunal.

LEVEL 2: SOCIAL SECURITY TRIBUNAL (GENERAL DIVISION)

The Social Security Tribunal (SST) is a court-like agency set up specifically for the Canada Pension Plan. The general division takes care of the next step in the appeals process, holding hearings run by its judges or panels.

On March 21, 2019, the federal government announced that general division hearings would go before a three-person panel (tribunal panel) rather than a tribunal judge. The panel will include a lawyer, a health professional, and a member of the public. These changes will happen from 2019 to 2023, so you may have a judge-alone hearing or a panel hearing, depending on when your case reaches the SST. As discussed in Chapter Three, you should present your case differently depending on the decision-maker.

Whether your hearing is with a judge or panel, it will look the same. It's like a trial, but not as formal. You'll give evidence, make opening statements, cross-examine witnesses (rarely), make closing arguments, and answer questions from the judge or panel members. The judge or panel will decide your appeal, so you need to present all your evidence here. Let's go over the steps for this level.

Step 1: Identify the deadline

You have ninety days to send your *notice of appeal* when you get your reconsideration denial, so you need to get out your calendar and count those days again. Nothing else matters if you miss the deadline, so make that deadline your top priority. We don't expect any changes with the ninety-day deadline.

Step 2: Send in the notice of appeal

Considering the government announcement on March 21, 2019, I expect some changes to the notice of appeal procedure and forms. Under the current system, you don't need to have your whole appeal package put together by the ninety-day deadline. You can send the official form to ask for the appeal, but then you have up to one year to send in the rest of your documents. You don't have to take the full year, but you have the time if you need it.

With the change to the tribunal panel, we expect the deadline for your documents to become shorter. You may even need to send all documents within the ninety-day deadline, and that means you must start as soon as you get that letter. It can take months to get critical documents that you need to win your appeal.

Given the expected changes, it's more important than ever to carefully read all letters you get from the Tribunal. These letters will have the deadlines that apply to you. Claimants often make mistakes on the notice of appeal form that need correcting before the ninety-day deadline, so keep an eye out for those letters. If you ignore them, you may never find out you made a mistake on your form. That will make you miss the ninety-day deadline, even though you sent your notice in time.

With tribunal judge hearings, when filing your notice of appeal, you have to choose whether you want an in-person hearing, video-conference hearing, teleconference hearing, or decision by document review only. We strongly recommend against the decision by document review. You should talk to and answer questions from the judge, so we recommend teleconference, video conference, or in-person hearings.

In my experience, you will get a faster hearing by teleconference or videoconference, because your case can go to the next available judge, regardless which province that judge is currently in. Many people, including lawyers, believe in-person hearings gain more approvals, but my team and I have done hundreds of appeals and seen no difference in the approval rates.

We don't know what the hearing choices will be for the new tribunal panel. Panel hearings may only be offered as in-person hearings, or you may have the same choices as the current tribunal judge system: in-person, teleconference, video-conference, or paper review only.

Step 3: Gather and send supporting documents

In the current system, you have up to one year to send in your documents and written submissions or *legal brief*. A legal brief will tell your story, using facts and law, to argue for your claim's approval. It must present a strong story that sways the judge or panel to rule in your favour, and you should send it last, after all your other documents. A solid legal brief will improve your odds of success.

With the move to the tribunal panel, we expect the deadline for your documents to become shorter. As noted above, you may need to send all documents within the ninety-day deadline for the notice of appeal. If that happens, then your document gathering will need to happen **before** you send in your notice. It can take months to get letters and records from doctors and other health professionals, so you must start immediately.

Many claimants don't send in important documents, don't respond to issues raised in earlier appeals, tell the wrong story, and send an ineffective legal brief. Any of these errors can make your appeal unwinnable, even if you qualify for benefits.

You should give as many of these documents as you can:

- All medical records needed for your approval
- Supplemental reports that address issues or gaps in information
- Employment records, including performance evaluations
- Rehabilitation records from any return-to-work program
- Education records for any retraining programs you tried

Step 4: Send the notice of readiness

After you send all your documents and legal brief, you can ask for a hearing with a *notice of readiness*. By sending this form, you're telling the tribunal you have no more documents to give and are ready for your hearing to be set.

We don't know if the notice of readiness will continue with the move to the tribunal panel. You'll need to pay attention to all letters and information sent to you by the Social Security Tribunal.

Step 5: Send any final reply submissions

The Tribunal gives Service Canada copies of all documents you send in for your appeal. Service Canada will then write their own legal brief and send in any new documents.

Once you get a copy of the Service Canada's legal brief, you have the choice to send a reply brief. As an add-on to your original brief, it has your response to any issues raised in Service Canada's legal brief that you didn't already cover, but sending a reply brief is not always the best strategy. Sometimes you should save it for the hearing. The best choice varies from case to case, so you have to use your judgment or ask your representative.

With the move to a tribunal panel, we don't know if you'll have the chance to respond in writing to the other side's legal brief.

Step 6: Attend your hearing

After you send in your notice of readiness, you'll get a date for your ninety-minute hearing. In this hearing, you need to tell the judge or panel your story and explain why they should overrule Service Canada's denial of your claim.

In planning your case, you need to focus on the key issues that will lead the judge or panel to approve your claim. Don't waste time talking about things that don't matter to them. Keep in mind, if you're representing yourself, that it's hard to be objective about your situation.

Your verbal testimony should support your written submissions, but don't just read your legal brief aloud, as that will annoy the judge or panel members.

Focus on the following:

- Personal information (age, family, living situation)
- Work history and experience
- Education and job skills
- How you tried to keep working
- Your disability and how it may have changed

- Past, current, and projected treatment
- Bad facts, such as getting fired or refusing treatment, and explanations for them

You must bring up any bad issues about your claim before anyone else does. Own your bad facts and tell the judge or panel why they don't matter, or it will look like you tried to hide them, which hurts your credibility.

Sometimes you simply need to admit that you made a mistake and have tried to fix it. For example, you can admit you refused a medication but changed your mind and began taking it. Your denial letter will usually highlight your bad facts, so read it carefully.

Step 7: Wait

Unfortunately, after all that, you won't get a decision right away. The judge or panel will issue a written decision within two months of the hearing, including the reasons for your approval or denial.

If the judge approves your claim, Service Canada will have ninety days to appeal that decision. This rarely happens. Usually Service Canada will process your claim and you'll get payment within three to six months.

If the judge or panel denies your claim, then you have the right to appeal the decision yourself.

LEVEL 3: SOCIAL SECURITY TRIBUNAL (APPEALS DIVISION)

The appeals division of the SST handles only appeals from the general division, not all appeals. We don't expect the new system changes to affect this level of appeal.

While the general division judge or panel will hear verbal testimony and decide based on the evidence, the appeals division only reviews the decision for errors in law, fact, or mixed fact and law. It won't accept new testimony or documents, focusing only on legal arguments and deciding whether the general division made an error of fact or law. Most importantly, you cannot change or re-tell your story – good or bad, you're stuck with how you've already presented your case.

This step of the appeals process goes beyond your personal claim, making it hard to go through without someone who has legal experience, like a lawyer. To win here, your side has to prove that the earlier judge made a serious error that doesn't follow the evidence or the law or both.

For example, I proved an error of fact in a case where, in denying the claim, the general division judge wrote that no doctor said the claimant couldn't work before the end of the qualifying period. However, a doctor did say my client was "incapable of work" in a report dated two months before the end of the period. This report was included in the documents for the general division hearing. We pointed out this document as the reason for our appeal.

We won, but only because the general division judge overlooked this report and didn't refer to it in the written decision. Had the judge mentioned the report and rejected the doctor's opinion, then we would've lost. Also, if we had failed to present this document at the general division hearing, then we would've lost because you can't add new evidence at this level of appeal.

Now let's take a look at the steps for this part of the process.

Step 1: Request leave to appeal to the SST (AD)

You don't have a right to this level of appeal. You only have the right to ask for permission to appeal, called requesting *leave to appeal*. You do this by filing yet another notice.

This time, you must identify critical errors of fact or law made by the judge or three-person panel in your last appeal. You can't nitpick little errors that make no difference. You have to present a mistake the judge or panel made that changed the outcome of the hearing. Acceptable grounds for this appeal have the judge:

- Not giving you a fair hearing.
- Committing an error of law.

- Making an error of fact without regard to the evidence.

- Committing an error of mixed fact and law.

The appeals division will review your notice and approve or deny your request.

Step 2: If granted, send your full appeal documents before the deadline

If the appeals division denies your request, then you can appeal this decision to deny leave to appeal, but such appeals have almost no chance of success. If the division grants your request, then you have forty-five days this time to send in a full appeal brief. Again, get out your calendar and make sure you mark the deadline.

Step 3: Wait

Once you send in your full appeal submissions, two things can happen. The appeals judge can make a decision based on the written submissions or schedule a hearing for verbal submissions as well. The verbal submissions are limited to the grounds of appeal set out in your written submissions. The appeals judge has the power to approve your claim or send it back for a new hearing with a judge or three-person panel.

LEVEL 4: FEDERAL COURT OF APPEAL

Any decision of the SST (AD) can go to the Federal Court of Appeal as an application for judicial review. These requests must happen within thirty days of receiving the unfavourable decision from the SST (AD). You start the process by filing a request for leave to appeal following the rules for the Federal Court of Appeal. If the court rejects your request, that ends it. You technically can appeal that decision to the Supreme Court of Canada, but such a request would have almost no chance of success, either.

If the court grants your request, then you have to send in your full appeal brief within the deadlines given by the court or set out in the rules of procedure. Like in the earlier step, this appeal only applies to a failure to give a fair hearing, errors of law, errors of fact, and errors of mixed fact and law. The Federal Court of Appeal can send your case back for a new hearing or can issue a final decision to approve or deny the claim.

Request for Extension

You have ninety days to appeal an unfavourable decision from Service Canada. This deadline starts the day you get the denial letter, not the date on the letter. If you can't send your appeal within that time, or if you already missed the deadline, then you can ask for an extension of time. You must ask for more time within one year of the missed deadline. The longer you wait, the more likely they are to say no.

Please note that Service Canada and the SST take deadlines seriously and will only grant extensions in a few situations. The Federal Court of Appeal created a system that adjudicators, judges, and panels must use when deciding to give an extension:

1. Has the person demonstrated a continuing intention to do the appeal? (Have you acted like someone who planned to appeal?)

2. Does the person have some chance of success? (Is your case unwinnable?)

3. Does the person have a reasonable excuse for the delay? (Did you have a good reason for missing the deadline?)

4. Will there be no prejudice to the other side if the extension is allowed? (Will this delay be unfair to the other side?)

The purpose of time extensions is to give fairness and justice for those appealing in good faith who missed the deadline for a good reason. It doesn't work for those who didn't do their best to make the deadline or say they didn't know about it, so make sure you read those letters and send in your papers!

Filing a New Application

If you don't get a time extension, you may have the choice to start over. You can even send in multiple applications, but if the SST gave a final decision on your claim, then you can't start a new claim with the same facts and DOO.

If your claim hasn't gone to the tribunal stage yet, then you can send in a new application with the same facts and DOO. However, remember that by sending in more than one application, you run the risk of mixing things up, which will hurt your credibility.

New Facts Applications

If you got a final decision from the tribunal, you may still have one tiny chance to have that decision reconsidered. To re-open a decision based on new facts, you need to show that you couldn't reasonably find the "new facts" before the hearing and these facts could affect the decision. These applications often fail because they present facts that the applicant could have found at the time of the hearing.

Summary Dismissals

The tribunal can summarily dismiss an appeal when it thinks the applicant has no reasonable chance of success. This step is harsh and rarely used. The summary dismissal is there to help valid claims get processed quickly and to keep the tribunal from getting swamped with hopeless claims, like those for workers who unfortunately become disabled before paying enough into the program. Summary dismissals also block claimants who keep sending in new applications, appeals, and lawsuits despite their lack of merit.

Common Reasons for Denial

If any of these common reasons for denial apply to you, then you should rethink your appeal, as you may waste time and effort for nothing. But if you think the reason given doesn't apply to you, then you'll want to know how to disprove it.

YOU DIDN'T PAY ENOUGH TO THE PROGRAM

Remember, you can only get CPP disability if you paid enough into the program at the time you became disabled. Even if they say you didn't pay enough, you still should have a disability lawyer look into it. You might get your application approved under the "late application" rules or other exceptions like pension credit splitting, credits from working in other countries, or the child rearing dropout provision. Another option is to continue working and making payments until you pay in enough. You could then reapply if you reach a point where you can no longer work due to disability.

YOUR DISABILITY ONSET FELL
OUTSIDE OF YOUR QUALIFYING PERIOD

Sometimes workers pay enough into the CPP but then stop working for other reasons before they become disabled. This situation makes it possible for a DOO to fall outside of the MQP. The usual qualifying periods end on the last date you paid into the program for four of the past six years, or three of the last six years if you have twenty-five years of contributions.

We recommend you consult a disability lawyer if you believe your DOO fell within the qualifying period although Service Canada says it didn't. You may qualify for extending your qualifying period, like if you left work to raise a child or became divorced or separated around that time. There may be other ways to prove your DOO fell within your MQP as well.

YOU MAKE AT LEAST $16K A YEAR

Simply put, if you make more than $16,029.96 a year (in 2018), then you make too much to qualify. This amount increases each year at the rate of inflation. To overcome this reason for denial, you need to show that your work situation was not "real" employment, like for an employer doing you a favour. If you're no longer working, you could show that the income came from a failed return to work but your disability kept you from holding the job.

YOU CAN'T DO YOUR OLD JOB
BUT CAN FIND A NEW ONE

It may hurt to lose your job to disability, but you have to try to find other work before applying for disability benefits. Your impairments have to keep you from working full- or part-time. To overcome this reason you have to try other jobs and show where you couldn't do them or couldn't keep them because of your disability.

YOU WERE LAID OFF,
BUT NOT BECAUSE OF DISABILITY

Adjudicators, judges, and panel members are always suspicious if a person starts a disability claim after being laid off from a job. If you got laid off before your disability stopped you from work, then you may have an uphill battle to qualify for CPP disability benefits.

However, sometimes you can show you were laid off because you were struggling with disability. Sometimes the layoff was a coincidence and you were planning on stopping work anyways. You may qualify to have a "severe and prolonged" disability even though you were technically still working when you were laid off.

I have helped clients win in all of these situations, but it was not easy. You'll need strong evidence and personal credibility to overcome the decision-maker's assumption that you only applied for disability because you lost your job.

YOU REFUSED A REASONABLE REQUEST

Yes, you can lose your benefits by not cooperating. If an adjudicator wants a copy of your complete medical file, then get that file in or risk denial. Refusing reasonable requests will raise a red flag.

If you fear something in your file will provoke a denial, you might as well take the chance that the decision-maker may disagree. Otherwise, you'll stay denied. To overcome this reason, tell the medical adjudicator you changed your mind and will now cooperate.

YOU DIDN'T TAKE REASONABLE MEDICAL ADVICE

You won't get CPP disability benefits if the medical records show you refused reasonable treatment recommendations. Remember, it's not what you consider reasonable but what the decision-makers consider reasonable. They base their decisions on the opinions of doctors and other experts in the medical records.

You must show that you left no stone unturned in the treatment of your disability. If your records show that you refused medications or dropped out of treatment programs early, then you'll lose your claim unless you have an acceptable excuse.

Acceptable excuses can include:

• Following the advice of one doctor over another.

• Avoiding treatments with high risk and low chance of success.

• A severe mental illness that prevents you from rational behavior.

• Inability to pay for treatment, after exhausting all ways for public funding.

These excuses must come with evidence, of course. You can probably find more, but this gives you an idea of what will and won't work.

YOU CAN'T FIND A JOB WHERE YOU LIVE

Unfortunately, the CPP program focuses on if you can do work in the national economy, not only your local area. If you can't find a job where you live, you have to look for work elsewhere and prove that you couldn't find a job you could do anywhere in Canada.

YOU CAN'T WORK NOW BUT MAY IN THE FUTURE

CPP only pays for "severe and prolonged" disability, not temporary disability. You could have a severe disability but have your claim denied because doctors expect you to get better after an upcoming medical procedure or treatment.

To overcome this reason, you would need to try the recommended treatment (to show it didn't work) or get a doctor to say the treatment isn't expected to get you back to work. Sometimes treatment will improve quality of life but not allow a person to work.

KEY TAKEAWAYS FOR THIS CHAPTER

♦ There are four levels of appeal: reconsiderations, general division tribunal hearings, appeals division tribunal hearings, and hearings at the Federal Court of Appeal.

♦ The general division tribunal hearings are currently run by a judge but will soon be run by a three-person panel that includes a lawyer, a health professional, and a member of the public.

♦ Each level of appeal is more complicated and has deadlines and procedures you must follow.

♦ Missing a deadline or failing to follow procedures can result in a final denial of your claim.

♦ The general division tribunal hearing with the judge or panel is your last chance to present evidence and tell the story of your claim.

♦ Hearings at the tribunal appeals division and Federal Court of Appeal focus only on whether the tribunal judge or panel made serious mistakes with the facts, laws, or procedural fairness.

♦ In some situations, you can start over with a new application if the general division tribunal judge or panel didn't issue a written decision denying your claim.

AFTER APPROVAL

When do payments start?

You should start receiving monthly payments within two to five months of approval. You'll get one letter from Service Canada confirming the approval, and then a second letter a few weeks later with a payment explanation sheet. This sheet gives you the amounts for your one-time retroactive payment and your monthly payments going forward. Service Canada will deposit the payments directly into your bank account.

How much will I get?

How much you get depends on how much you paid in. The average monthly payment in 2018 was $971.23, the maximum payment was $1,335.83, and the children's payment was $244.64 per child. These amounts increase every year for inflation. For example, if you qualify for the average CPP disability payment and have two children under age eighteen, then you would get $971 (disability) + $244 (child 1) + $244 (child 2) = $1,459 per month.

What about taxes?

CPP disability benefits, both monthly and retroactive, are taxable as income. The one-time retroactive payment can sometimes cause tax issues. In some cases, Revenue Canada will tax the entire sum in the year you got it. In others, Revenue Canada will tax you on the part of the lump sum that went directly to your insurance company.

If your retroactive payment gets paid out over two or more years, then you can ask Revenue Canada to divide it by those years and tax the funds as you get them. This spreads out the taxation and keeps that sum in a lower tax bracket in each of those years.

Tax issues can also come up when some or all of the CPP retroactive payment goes to an insurer as reimbursement for past disability insurance payments. Known as a long-term disability (LTD) benefits overpayment, it usually plays out in one of two ways.

If your LTD benefits were taxable, then the CPP benefit paid to the insurer will not be taxed. When issuing your annual T4A for LTD benefits, your insurer will include the reimbursement as an offset, a deduction against income on your T4A. This reduces your taxable income by the same amount.

If for some reason your insurer doesn't adjust the T4A to include the reimbursement, then you can still claim it as a deduction at line 232 of your individual tax return. You can't claim the deduction twice, so be careful not to include it at line 232 if it appears on your T4A from the insurer. Consult a tax expert for advice on this.

A more difficult situation arises when your LTD benefits are non-taxable. Your insurance company won't issue a T4A, and you can't claim the retroactive payment as a deduction. Revenue Canada will tax the retroactive payment, but you can reduce your burden.

First, ask Revenue Canada to spread the tax on the payment over the years you would have gotten the payments. This creates smaller sums over two or more years and puts you in a lower tax bracket. Second, you can apply for the disability tax credit. If approved, the credit may cut down your taxes for the retroactive payment.

What's an overpayment?

Winning your CPP claim may put you in an overpayment situation if you get disability benefits from other sources, including LTD, workers compensation, or provincial social assistance payments. These other benefit payers can cut back what they pay you by the same amount you get from CPP, including both the retroactive payment and the monthly payments.

If these other payments covered months covered by the retroactive payment, then you'll owe that to the other payer. Remember, you must tell all other disability benefit payers of the amount of your CPP payment, or you may get charged with fraud. You should send each a copy of the payment explanation sheet Service Canada sends before your first CPP payment.

What if I have other income?

Non-employment income sources have no effect on your monthly disability payments. Common sources include RRSPs, TFSAs, pension income, rental income, capital gains, LTD benefits, royalty income, and more. They key is whether you're earning money from work, including self-employment.

Your CPP disability payments only drop if you earn more than $5,500 (in 2018) in employment or self-employment income. This amount increases each year at the rate of inflation. Once you start earning more than $5,500 or demonstrate the ability to earn more than $5,500, then your CPP disability benefit may drop or stop altogether.

Can I go back to work?

You have an obligation to tell the CPP disability program if you start earning more than $5,500 per year (in 2018). If you earn $5,500 or less, then you can continue to get your full disability payment.

You can also apply for the CPP Disability Vocational Rehabilitation Program. This program offers free services to help you get back to work, including paying for college. You can continue to get your disability benefit during the vocational program and as you begin work again.

Your benefits would only stop once you earn more than $16,029.96 per year (in 2018). This amount also increases each year at rate of inflation. If you go back to work but your disability returns within two years, then your benefits restart without a new application. If your disability returns within three to five years, you can apply for a fast-track application.

If something changes, how do I handle it?

You should inform the program of any new changes in your medical condition, treatment, or employment. Service Canada may also review your claim to confirm your ongoing eligibility for benefits. Don't worry, that doesn't mean you did something wrong. It's a normal part of the process. If your taxable income crosses the $5,500 threshold, Service Canada may open a review.

Service Canada has access to your taxable earnings, so you should report that your situation has changed rather than waiting for someone to notice. A review can take many forms but usually involves a phone interview with the medical adjudicator, an update of your medical records, an updated report from your doctor, and possibly updated information from your new job.

Remember, you should always tell Service Canada if your situation changes. Don't withhold information because you're afraid of a review. Withholding information can look like you're trying to commit fraud, even if you're not.

What if I move or go on vacation?

You can travel outside of Canada as much as you like, as long as Service Canada has your current contact information. You may also have to show Service Canada how you'll continue your medical care while out of the country, especially if you don't return for months or years. And you need a way to get mail from Service Canada. If you don't let Service Canada know how to reach you while you're out of the country, you may lose your benefits.

KEY TAKEAWAYS FOR THIS CHAPTER

♦ You can expect payments to start two to five months after approval.

♦ Your payment amount is based on your contribution history.

♦ The maximum payment was $1,335.83 in 2018 and increases each year at the rate of inflation.

♦ Your first payment includes your monthly benefit amount, plus a one-time retroactive payment for past benefits owed.

♦ If you've gotten disability-related payments from other sources (e.g., insurance, social services), you may owe some (or all) of the retroactive CPP payment to those other payers.

♦ CPP disability benefits are taxable as income.

♦ Keep Service Canada informed of any changes to your medical condition or contact information.

REPRESENTATION

Authorized Representative

Both Service Canada and the Social Security Tribunal allow a claimant to have an *authorized representative*, or AR. The AR helps you during your claim or appeal and can sign certain documents and forms for you. But don't confuse an authorized representative with an authorized person, who can get communications from Service Canada or the tribunal. An authorized person can't act on your behalf or make decisions about your claim or appeal.

For your AR, Service Canada allows a lawyer, guardian, curator, trustee, committee, executor, power of attorney, or any other legal representative. The AR must be appointed under the laws of Canada to manage your affairs, and you must give legal documents confirming this appointment. These legal documents include a mandate, trusteeship, power of attorney documents, and letterhead from a lawyer confirming representation or an official CPP program form.

The SST defines a representative as anyone appointed to assist a claimant during the tribunal appeal process. You appoint an AR by sending the official form given by the SST. Anyone who assists you at the hearing and charges a fee must follow provincial law rules. But anyone who is not a lawyer or paralegal licensed in your province may be breaking the law and should not represent you at the hearing.

Negligent Representation

All ARs must meet the same legal standard of competence regardless of their education, training, or experience. If your representative makes a negligent mistake that results in the denial of your claim or appeal, you can start a *malpractice claim* to try to win back the money you would have gotten from the CPP disability program.

Negligence includes missing deadlines, poor case work, failure to give key information, or even weak advocacy. Some of these items can be hard to prove, though.

You should also know that some representatives mean well but still give negligent service because they don't know enough to represent people in CPP disability claims and appeals. This can happen with both licensed and unlicensed representatives, but you take a greater risk with an unlicensed representative because they likely have no malpractice insurance and are usually not governed by a code of ethics or rules of professional responsibility.

Licensed and Unlicensed Representatives

Licensed representatives include lawyers in all provinces and paralegals in provinces that license paralegals. Unlicensed representatives are often referred to as non-attorney advocates or non-lawyer advocates.

You need to know the differences between licensed and unlicensed. Licensed representatives have formal credentials in the law, the legal process, and legal advocacy. They must follow a strict code of ethics and rules of professional responsibility. They must also carry malpractice insurance that would pay you if they make mistakes handling your claim or appeal.

Unlicensed representatives have varying degrees of education and practical experience, but usually no formal credentials in the law or advocacy. They usually aren't governed by codes of ethics and rules of professional responsibility and probably don't have malpractice insurance.

I'm not saying that you should avoid all non-licensed representatives. There are many who have a high level of competence and are passionate about the work they do. Also, a license doesn't guarantee a win for your claim. You really need to do your homework when choosing an AR.

However, the key difference is the accountability. You're protected if a licensed representative makes a mistake, but you don't know what you may wind up in if a non-licensed representative makes a mistake.

Paid and Unpaid Representatives

Obviously, paid representatives make their paycheques by representing people in claims and appeals. They can include both licensed and unlicensed individuals and businesses.

You can negotiate the terms of payment to include a flat fee, fees based on time spent working on the claim or appeal, or a contingency fee, also known as a no-win, no-fee agreement. No-win no-fee means that the representative doesn't get paid unless you do, so he or she has a vested interest in winning your claim.

Unpaid representatives include individuals, groups, and non-profit organizations that offer advocacy and representation as part of their mandate. These organizations normally use non-licensed advocates to assist people with CPP disability claims, but some use licensed lawyers and paralegals.

Many such groups and organizations give good quality representation, but remember that they don't have to follow the same rules that lawyers and paralegals do. However, the non-profit organization may have insurance to pay you if their volunteer or employee doesn't handle your appeal properly.

Do you need a representative?

Let me be clear. You can lose a winnable case if you make mistakes and don't present the claim properly. Too many claimants believe the "truth of the situation" holds more power than it really does.

Regardless of how disabled you have become, the decision-makers can only judge your situation by the documents and testimony you officially give. If you don't show the truth of your situation in your documents and testimony, you will lose your claim, no matter how much you deserve to win.

Many claims need you to take a strategic approach to gathering and presenting your evidence. For example, if you applied under the late applicant clause, then you need to get medical records that cover the times in question. In such a case, relying on current medical records will result in a denial.

Successful lawyers know that the best story wins the case. For over two thousand years, lawyers have known about the link between good storytelling and successful advocacy. Your case is a story, and you have to tell a good one, a believable one. Your story must be authentic and account for all the facts, both good and bad.

A high-quality advocate has a lot more practice than you at telling the story needed to win your claim, so you should consider hiring this expert to tell your story. Remember, your story should be convincing for the decision-makers, rather than just what you believe is convincing or important. You have to focus on seeing things from the decision-makers' point of view.

Do you remember the upset woman in the preface of this book? She lost her hearing just before the creation of the Social Security Tribunal (SST), so she got a second chance for a hearing with the new tribunal. When she hired me, I sent in new documents and presented her story differently. Upon getting copies of the new documents and our legal brief, Service Canada offered to approve her case before the hearing. They now saw the case differently and believed they would lose at the new hearing, so they approved the claim. This is the power of the right evidence and a compelling story.

In another case, a woman approached me to represent her mother. They were desperate because their tribunal hearing was only a few weeks away but their representative had called their case "unwinnable" and withdrawn. I explained the situation to the Tribunal, and they granted us a time extension so I could give new documents and a legal brief. I adjusted the case story and filled the evidence gaps. There were challenges with proving disability, but the client was very authentic. She had a compelling story just waiting to be told. We then won the case at the tribunal hearing.

Both of these examples show the importance of sending in the right evidence and telling the right story. Along with your credibility, you must get these two things right. And you can easily lose a winnable case if you get any one of these things wrong.

If you need to stand before the Tribunal, I strongly recommend a licensed representative with demonstrated competence in CPP disability appeals. The tribunal hearing is your **last chance to give evidence** in support of your claim, your last chance to decide how to **tell your story**. If you lose because the tribunal didn't see key evidence or found your story unconvincing, you won't get a second chance to fix things.

I understand that you have to worry about the cost. But remember, some representatives only get paid when (and if) you get paid. If you win your claim, it may cost up to thirty-three percent of the retroactive payment (plus taxes). The fees, case-related expenses, and taxes could total forty-percent of the retroactive payment. But you would keep the rest of the retroactive payment and all of the future payments.

Depending on your age, the value of the future payments can greatly exceed the amount of the retroactive payment. So, you need to ask yourself if you can afford up to forty percent of the retroactive payment to give yourself a better chance of getting sixty percent of the retroactive payment and one hundred percent of all future payments.

You can also explore options for getting an unpaid representative from a non-profit legal clinic or organization. Remember that representatives are not all the same. They can have varying amounts of experience and credentials. You need to find out if any such organization exists in your local area.

Some claimants believe that if they lose the general division hearing, they can hire a representative to handle the appeals division hearing. You can, but the general division hearing was your last chance to submit evidence and tell your story. Identifying the missing evidence and telling a convincing story is the highest value a representative can give you, but you have to make these things happen before the appeals division hearing.

After the general division hearing, the focus is on whether the tribunal judge or panel made serious mistakes with the information presented to them. A representative can help figure out if you have grounds for appeal.

KEY TAKEAWAYS FOR THE CHAPTER

- ◆ Service Canada and the Tribunal allow you to have an authorized representative to help with your claim or appeals.

- ◆ Authorized representatives can be licensed or unlicensed.

- ◆ Licensed representatives must have malpractice insurance and follow a strict code of ethics and rules of professional conduct.

- ◆ Poor representation can result in a denial of an otherwise winnable claim.

- ◆ You should consider a representative for your general division hearing, because it's your last chance to present evidence and tell your story.

- ◆ Choose your representative carefully.

Glossary

This glossary, arranged in alphabetical order, covers most if not all of the terms you may have trouble with. When you see a term in the guide in *italics*, you'll find it here in the glossary.

Adjudication – Process of reviewing a claim and deciding to approve or deny it.

Appeal – Process of asking a decision-maker with more authority than the first to overturn a claim denial.

Authorized representative – Person legally appointed to assist a claimant during a claim or appeal.

Benevolent employment situation – Setup where an employer pays a person out of friendship or charity rather than for work done in the job.

Child-rearing dropout provision – Rule that allows a primary caregiver for a child under the age of seven to get contribution credits for years out of the workforce.

Claimant – Person applying for CPP disability benefits.

Contribution requirements – Amount a person must contribute to CPP to qualify for its disability benefits.

Credit splitting – CPP rule that allows divorced or separated spouses to share in each other's CPP pension credits.

Date of onset (DOO) – Designated date when disability became "severe and prolonged" as defined by the CPP program.

Decision-makers – Service Canada agent, tribunal judge, or three-person panel who will approve or deny the disability claim or appeal.

Documents – All records and written submissions to the tribunal, including electronic and paper records.

Late applicant provision – Rule that allows a person to apply for benefits outside of the minimum qualifying period (MQP). However, the date of onset of disability must still fall within the MQP.

Leave to appeal – Official request for permission to appeal.

Legal brief – Written submissions to the judge that tells a claimant's story to argue for approval. It will set out the facts and law and apply the law to the facts.

Malpractice claim – Lawsuit against a representative who makes a negligent mistake that results in the denial of a claim or appeal.

Medical adjudicator – Service Canada agent who reviews CPP disability claims and decides to approve or deny them.

Minimum qualifying period (MQP) – Time during which a person made the minimum amount of payments into the CPP program, usually four years in a six-year window, to qualify for disability benefits. Also, the date of onset of disability must happen during this period.

Notice of appeal – Official written notice sent to the tribunal to ask for an appeal of a denial.

Notice of readiness – Step in the appeals process where a person sends a written statement to the Tribunal to say he or she is ready to schedule a hearing.

Panel (Three-person tribunal panel) – The lawyer, health professional, and member of the public appointed to the tribunal to conduct hearings as a unit and decide to approve or deny appeals.

Prolonged – Defined by the CPP Act as "likely to be long, continued and of indefinite duration, or is likely to result in death".

Reconsideration – First level of appeal for a denied claim. A new adjudicator will review the claim to reconsider the first denial.

Severe – Defined by the CPP Act as "incapable regularly of pursuing any substantially gainful occupation".

Social Security Tribunal – Administrative law court established to conduct hearings and decide to approve or deny claims.

Submissions – Written or verbal information given to help the decision-maker reach a decision.

Tribunal member – Administrative law judge appointed to the Social Security Tribunal. Tribunal members conduct hearings and decide to approve or deny appeals.

Made in the USA
Columbia, SC
20 May 2022

60676166R00039